An American Bird Conservancy
Compact Guide

Paul Lehman
Ornithological Editor

CONTENTS

COASTAL BIRD HABITAT

IDENTIFYING WATERBIRDS

CHECKLIST AND INDEX

COASTAL BIRD HABITAT

by
EDWARD S. BRINKLEY

Waterbirds along the Atlantic and Gulf coasts spend their lives in a world dominated by the ebb and flow of tides. Most people don't consider the tides when going out to see birds, but tides can make the difference between seeing many species and coming up empty-handed.

An area of open water devoid of bird life at one time of day may be transformed into a mudflat teeming with birds only a few hours later. Low or falling tides are critical feeding times for many coastal birds because their prey—mostly small marine organisms—are exposed or covered by much less water, making them easier to hunt.

By contrast, high spring tides are sometimes the best time to search for those elusive chicken-like marsh dwellers known as rails. Usually they skulk about unnoticed in the interior of a marsh. At the highest tides, they are concentrated into the high, dry, and more open marsh borders.

It helps to understand how tides work. Each day, largely because of the revolution of the moon around the earth, there are two high and two low tides, at least at most locations. The moon's orbital speed also determines that there is a daily shift of about 50 minutes in the

Want to Help Conserve Birds?

It's as Easy as ABC!

By becoming a member of the American Bird Conservancy, you can help ensure work is being done to protect many of the species in this field guide. You can receive *Bird Conservation* magazine quarterly to learn about bird conservation throughout the Americas and *World Birdwatch* magazine for information on international bird conservation.

Make a difference to birds.
Copy this card and mail to the address listed below.

☐ **Yes,** I want to become a member and receive *Bird Conservation* magazine.
A check in the amount of $18 is enclosed.

☐ **Yes,** I want to become an International member of ABC and receive both *Bird Conservation* and *World Birdwatch* magazines.
A check in the amount of $40 is enclosed.

NAME
_____

ADDRESS
_____

CITY/STATE/ZIP CODE
_____

Return to: American Bird Conservancy
1250 24th Street NW, Suite 400; Washington, DC 20037
or call **1-888-BIRD-MAG** or e-mail: abc@abcbirds.org

Memberships are tax deductible to the extent allowable by law.

The **American Bird Conservancy (ABC)** is a U.S.-based, not-for-profit organization formed to unify bird conservation efforts across the Americas and dedicated to the conservation of birds throughout the Western Hemisphere. ABC practices conservation through partnership, bringing together the partners whose expertise and resources are best suited to each task.

The ABC **Policy Council** has a membership of more than 70 organizations sharing a common interest in the conservation of birds. Composed of ornithologists, policy specialists, educators, and general bird enthusiasts, the Council is a professional forum for exchanging information and discussing critical and emerging bird conservation issues. The Council provides policy and scientific advice to conservationists, stimulates a network of support for conservation policies through national, state, and local groups, and directly accomplishes conservation through ABC.

ABC is a working member of **Partners in Flight (PIF)**, an Americas-wide coalition of more than 150 organizations and government agencies dedicated to bird conservation. Initially begun to find ways to reverse the decline in neotropical migratory bird species, PIF has broadened its scope to include all non-game birds in the Americas. PIF links birders, hunters, government, industry, landowners, and other citizens in a unified effort to conserve bird populations and habitats.

Many North American "birds" found in this guide spend more than half their lives in Latin America and the Caribbean. The needs for bird conservation in this region are at least as great as in the U.S. Through PIF, ABC is building U.S. support for capable, but often underfunded, conservation partners throughout the Americas.

PIF's bird conservation strategy, called the **Flight Plan**, can be obtained from ABC, the National Fish and Wildlife Foundation, or the U.S. Fish and Wildlife Service. PIF's National Coordinator serves on ABC's staff, and ABC helps implement the Flight Plan through its Important Bird Areas (IBA) initiative. ABC members receive *Bird Conservation*, the magazine about PIF and American bird conservation.

Designed by Jack L. Griggs & Peg Alrich

Edited by Virginia Croft

Illustrations reformatted by John E. Griggs
from the original illustrations published in
All the Birds of North America
by the following artists:

Jonathan Alderfer pp. 53-61, 65-83, 99-119;
John Dawson p. 120; Alan Messer p. 63;
Hans Peeters pp. 85-97; Bart Rulon p. 31;
Barry Van Dusen pp. 33-51.

All the Waterbirds: Atlantic and Gulf Coasts
Copyright © 1999 by Jack L. Griggs. All rights reserved.

FIRST EDITION

Library of Congress Cataloging-in-Publication Data

Griggs, Jack L.
    All the water birds. Atlantic and Gulf Coasts / Jack L. Griggs.
        p.   cm.
    Includes index.
    ISBN 0-06-273653-1
    1. Water birds—Atlantic Coast (North America)—Identification. 2. Water
birds—Gulf Coast (U.S.)—Identification. 3. Water birds—Gulf Coast
(Mexico)—Identification. I. Title
QL681.G773   1999
598.176'0975—dc21   98-41932

99 00 01 02 03 ❖/PE 6 5 4 3 2 1

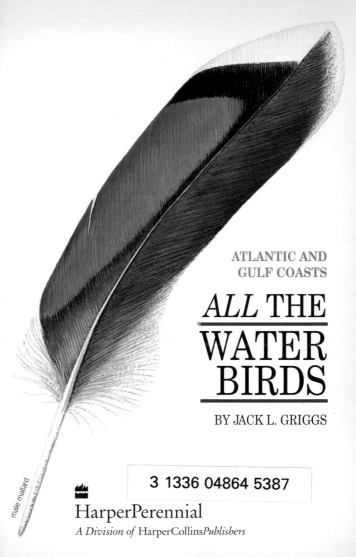

male mallard

ATLANTIC AND
GULF COASTS

ALL THE
WATER
BIRDS

BY JACK L. GRIGGS

HarperPerennial

A Division of HarperCollins*Publishers*

SUN

EARTH   or

MOON

SPRING TIDES

SUN

MOON   EARTH

NEAP TIDES

timing of the tides, so that if you know that one high tide is at 3:00 p.m. today, you can estimate that it will be around 3:50 p.m. tomorrow.

If the sun is aligned with the moon and earth, the highest and lowest tides are created, called spring tides. When the sun and moon are at right angles with respect to the earth, tidal change is much smaller, and these are known as neap tides. These tidal cycles complete themselves every two weeks. Checking a local tide table is an excellent way to begin a coastal birding adventure.

Tidal activity varies tremendously from place to place. The tidal activity and the kind of substrate—mud, sand, or stone—that makes up a shoreline or flat determines what sort of organisms will be found there and thus also what birds will come to feed.

Along the northeastern coast, tidal currents can be very strong, with differences between high and low tide of as much as 50 feet at some places in Nova Scotia! Such a strong surge means that smaller particles of stone and sand are regularly washed away from coastlines.

Some of the New England coastlines are entirely stony, composed of granite, often in the form of pebbles, derived from the wearing down of ancient rocks. In the mid-Atlantic

9

ROCK CRAB
to 5"

RED CHITON
to 1"

BLUE MUSSELS
to 4"

and southeastern states, white sand (calcite or calcium carbonate) beaches are found.

Sand is mostly shell, finely ground by the relentless surf. From this softer, more pliable substance, the milder tides of the South create barrier islands and sandy capes—wonderful places to observe bird life. In the Gulf of Mexico, where tides are the most moderate (only a few feet at most), beaches also contain varying amounts of coral from the coral reefs offshore.

The intertidal zone is the area between high and low water marks. The Northeast's intertidal zone is a dynamic and sometimes harsh environment that nevertheless supports a great variety of seaweed (species of algae) on its rocky shores. Within this vegetation and on the rocks themselves, marine life proliferates. Crustaceans, shellfish with segmented bodies, are especially numerous along shorelines.

Small crustaceans such as the Jonah crab and rock crab scurry among the vegetation and are prey to gulls and larger shorebirds. Shellfish of other types cling to rocks and pilings; most are mollusks with soft, unsegmented bodies, like oysters and snails. Blue mussels are common and an important food for gulls and sea ducks. Sandpipers take many smaller "bivalves," that is, mollusks with two parts to the shell.

NORTHERN ROCK BARNACLE
to 1"

CLAM WORM
to 8"

Animals with a single hard shell fall into many classifications, and almost all of them, including dogwinkles, limpets, chitons, and barnacles, look like dinner to a hungry seabird. Purple sandpipers are specialists on the rocks and seaweed of the intertidal zone. Turnstones join them there and sometimes sanderlings. Some gulls occasionally forage in the seaweed and at tidal pools, taking anything from shellfish to sea urchins to whatever dead sea creature has washed ashore.

The extensive silty mudflats that are exposed on northern coasts during low tides are good places to find shorebirds. Here sandpipers and plovers in countless shimmering masses come to feed on the variety of small marine organisms in the mud and shallow tidal pools. The bills of the different sandpipers are of varying lengths and shapes, so that all areas and levels of a mudflat are exploited.

Many of the tiny prey gleaned from the surface by small-billed birds like the least sandpiper are too small for an observer to see. Likewise, it is usually impossible to see the prey caught by the sandpipers that probe into the mud. Sometimes, however, a worm can be seen pulled from its burrow like a strand of spaghetti.

Marine worms such as clam worms and mud worms tunnel though coastal mud much like

TUBE MAKER
(AN AMPHIPOD)
to ³/₁₆"

the familiar earthworm. They are a prolific source of food for shorebirds. The whimbrel is partial to large worms known as sipunculids. "Amphipods," also abundant on mudflats, are tiny crustaceans without hard shells that provide food for dozens of waterbird species.

Above the high water line, some birds wait out the high tide on rocks. Oceanic species such as the Atlantic puffin, razorbill, and black guillemot nest in crevices between rocks above the high water line on northerly New England coasts and in the Canadian Maritimes.

**GANNETS
PLUNGE-DIVING**

Where rocks are flatter, sometimes with sandy soils and vegetation on them, terns such as the common and roseate may establish nesting colonies. Even snowy egrets, which typically nest in small trees on the mid-Atlantic coast, have nested on rocky islands off the coast of Maine, so keep a sharp eye out for the unusual!

The open water beyond the low tide mark is where the majority of birds feed on the northern coasts. This area is still affected by tides but is never exposed during low tide. In this environment, well within sight of shore, great varieties of birds forage. Some are aerialists that feed by picking from the surface or plunge-diving (diving from flight). Others are swimmers that dive from the surface.

Fish is their most common food. Small fish like capelin and sand lance provide prey for most species. Gannets take larger fish like the widespread menhaden. These "bait" fish are sometimes driven to the water's surface by predatory fish such as striped bass and blue-fish. A large flock of seabirds actively feeding in a small area of water often indicates that larger fish are feeding below.

Many swimmers, such as the eiders and scoters, dive to feed on beds of mussels, clams, and similar mollusks. Anyone who has eaten shellfish will marvel in watching an eider break open a mussel in its bill, with apparently no more effort than a person might use to shell a peanut!

Just offshore there are often tidelines or rips visible, areas where outgoing tides have con-centrated flotsam along distinct, winding, foamy lines. Bonaparte's gulls, among other birds, feed actively in these tidelines and at sewage outflows.

The intertidal zones of more southerly beaches are generally smaller, only a few yards wide in some places, but even here the resident marine organisms must cope with periods of immersion and exposure. Birds find an abundant variety of prey on which to feed at low tide.

MOLE CRAB
to 1"

**TELLINS AND
COQUINAS**
to 7/8"

GHOST CRAB
to 2"

Herring gulls can often be seen stamping their feet in the moist sand to find mole crabs. Mole crabs are found from the Chesapeake Bay southward. They are the oval-shaped inch-long or smaller creatures that are seen constantly burrowing back into wet sand after being exhumed by waves. Many shorebirds also feed heavily on mole crabs and their larvae.

Clams of many species and sizes are eagerly sought by shorebirds, which capture them when the clams' bodies are extended outside the open shell. Tiny clams like coquinas and tellins are important resources for long-distance migrants. The larger razor clam is prized by the American oystercatcher.

Among the gems of birding in the mid-Atlantic are the shallow beaches of Delaware Bay, which in May become covered with the tiny eggs of horseshoe crabs. This attracts millions of birds, from the local laughing and ring-billed gulls to arctic nesters such as red knots, turnstones, and sanderlings, all eager to fatten up on the protein-rich eggs on their way to nesting areas far to the north.

Above the intertidal zone on sandy beaches along the entire coast, one finds lines of de-bris called wrack, in which various birds (and ghost crabs) may forage on sand fleas, flies, and larvae. Sand fleas, often called beach

14

SAND FLEAS
about 1"

hoppers, are not fleas but small crustaceans favored by piping plovers and other shore-birds of the upper beach. Ghost crabs are prey of larger birds, including herons, which sometimes forage on open beaches.

Turnstones and plovers often pick through beach wrack, as do crows and boat-tailed grackles, both landbirds. Crows along the coast are not all the same. They look about the same, but the American crow gives the familiar *caw*, whereas fish crows give a nasal double-noted *eh-eh*. The boat-tailed grackle has a dis-tinctively long tail. Males are a dark, iridescent blue; females are smaller and dingy brown.

♂
♀

BOAT-TAILED GRACKLE

Beyond the intertidal zone in mid-Atlantic and southern waters, one sees a diversity of feeding waterbirds. Look for pelicans, gan-nets, and a handful of different terns. Great numbers of brown pelicans can now be seen along beaches from Delaware to the Gulf of Mexico. Pelicans, like their relatives the gan-nets, which replace them in winter in the mid-Atlantic states, plunge-dive for fish that school mostly in the inshore waters. The double-crested cormorant also preys on schooling fish and sometimes gathers in large numbers.

Offshore in the mid-Atlantic, grebes, gannets, and diving ducks concentrate in winter and during migration. In spring and early summer,

15

adult

young

BALD EAGLES

OSPREY

oceanic migrants like the sooty shearwater and Wilson's storm-petrel can sometimes be seen from shore. Even waterbirds that don't forage in the open ocean migrate along the immediate coastline in spring and fall.

Other species sometimes seen from the shoreline are the parasitic jaeger (in migration) and the magnificent frigatebird (south of the Carolinas). Both birds are experts at stealing fish from other seabirds, especially terns, but they may also snatch up an exhausted land-bird migrant if the opportunity presents itself.

Hunting for fish off the shoreline isn't limited to seabirds. Fish-eating raptors such as osprey and even the bald eagle are seen more and more often along the beaches. Their popula-tions, like those of the brown pelican, were nearly wiped out by pesticide poisoning in the 1950s and 1960s, but their numbers continue to rise in the 1990s.

Bald eagles are well known for their white heads and tails, but young birds have dark heads and dark-banded tails. Ospreys can be recognized in flight at a good distance by their wing shape and bold underwing pattern. The wing shape is gull-like. Note how the leading edge of the wing projects forward at the wrist, unlike the wings of the bald eagle or other raptors. The projection is emphasized by

16

the black patch at the wrist contrasting with the white underbody.

In late fall migration, watch for falcons, especially the peregrine falcon and the merlin, as they course high overhead or zip along the dune lines hunting small shorebirds and migrating landbirds, which often concentrate along coasts.

MERLIN

Because they fly so fast, falcons can be hard to identify without experience. Their flight, swift and direct, is a helpful mark. The gleaming white breast of the peregrine is a good mark. The merlin's color varies with sex and region, but all are streaked below and have a dark tail with pale bands and a whitish tip.

PEREGRINE FALCON

Sheltered inlets and bays occur where rivers, streams, and creeks flow into the ocean. These coastal areas are not exposed to the open ocean and the beating of the waves and provide many bird-friendly habitats. Estuaries are the areas where rivers and streams meet the ocean. The mixture of freshwater and saltwater masses makes for a unique environment of low-salinity water called brackish water.

Extensive marshes often form near river mouths and on the border of bays, and because high tides push marine water well up into the river, these are known as tidal marshes or salt marshes.

17

COMMON PERIWINKLES
to 1"

Salt marshes, and estuarine systems generally, are nurseries to many species of birds and also the fish and other diverse aquatic organisms on which the birds prey. The organisms are similar to those found in open mudflats, but salt marshes also provide fare such as fiddler crabs, periwinkles, and an abundance of seeds and aquatic vegetation.

Periwinkles—mollusks with pale snail-like shells—cling to marsh grasses. Male sand fiddler and mud fiddler crabs are often seen battling each other with their single outsized claws, but much of the larvae and "zoea" on which birds feed are so small as to go undetected by people who visit.

Waterfowl are the primary consumers of marsh vegetation, and in winter, the protected coastal waters of the Atlantic and Gulf of Mexico are home to tens of millions of geese, swans, and dabbling ducks (those, such as mallards, pintails, and teal, that feed on surface vegetation or by tipping up to reach plants on shallow bottoms). In the mid-Atlantic states, with patience and luck, most of the native species of waterfowl can be observed in a small area of bay and marsh and adjacent ocean in just a morning's outing!

Horned and pied-billed grebes also winter in bays near salt marshes, and brant are closely

FIDDLER CRAB
to 2"

18

SHRIMP LARVAE
to 1/4"

tied to salt marsh habitats with abundant eelgrass and similar aquatic vegetation. They, along with tundra swans, American wigeons, canvasbacks, and other species that rely heavily on such plant matter, have seriously declined in many areas with damaged ecosystems. Canvasbacks have recovered from such losses in part by switching from aquatic plants to a diet consisting mostly of fish in some areas.

Great varieties of shorebirds make use of salt marshes and their related tidal pools and mudflats through the winter and in spring and fall migrations. Many migrate at night and spend the daytime busily refueling.

On deep bays and inlets, diving ducks such as canvasbacks, redheads, buffleheads, and scaup often gather in large mixed flocks known as rafts. Diving ducks also raft on the open ocean, often over shellfish beds.

CRAB ZOEA
to 1/8"

Terns, rails, laughing gulls, the willet, and some ducks raise their young in food-rich estuaries. Belted kingfishers also forage here, preferring the quiet waters of marshes and streams to the turbulent ocean. Forster's and gull-billed terns are likely to be seen coursing over marshes hunting insects and fish. In tall marsh, an observer may hear the quiet *coo-coo-coo-coo* call of the least bittern. With patience, bitterns are occasionally seen.

19

If small oak, pine, or myrtle trees are available next to marshes, several species of herons, egrets, and ibises may nest in dense colonies and forage around the clock in the marshes, each species feeding in a slightly different area or depth of marsh on slightly different species or sizes of fish.

MARSH WREN

Landbirds also nest in salt marshes. Red-winged blackbirds are common. Some sparrows nest exclusively in salt marsh, including the saltmarsh sharp-tailed and the seaside sparrow. The sparrows are somewhat secretive (see *All the Birds of North America*), as is another salt marsh dweller, the marsh wren. The marsh wren has the stubby, cocked tail and curved bill characteristic of wrens. Its best marks are the white eyebrow, unstreaked crown, and rusty back.

BARN OWL

Predators such as barn owls and the harrier can be found most of the year in temperate marshes. The barn owl's heart-shaped facial disc is distinctive. For the harrier, foraging style is a helpful mark. Harriers fly low and buoyantly over marshes, holding their wings in a shallow V. They hunt for rodents by sight and sound. Females are brown above; males, gray. Both sexes have distinctive white rumps.

HARRIER

Salt marshes also form on the sheltered sides of barrier islands. The sides facing the open ocean are typically flat, sandy beaches that can be home to large colonies of terns, skimmers, gulls, plovers, willets, and oyster-catchers. Fish crows and some of the larger gulls patrol these colonies and scavenge eggs and nestlings when possible.

Harriers and horned larks nest on sandy islands over much of the Atlantic coast, and in winter, they are joined by snow buntings, short-eared owls, and even the rare snowy owl.

HORNED LARK

Horned larks have a distinctive face pattern even when the "horns" are flattened. Snow buntings are sparrow-like birds seen in flocks. In winter, they blend into a dry sand background. In flight, they show a lot of white in the wings. Short-eared owls hunt like harriers, but usually at dusk or on overcast days. They are a tawny brown, with dark marks at the bend of the wings visible in flight. The "ears" are seldom visible; the head appears round.

SHORT-EARED OWL

Very large rivers like the Mississippi move enormous amounts of fresh water and sediment into marine environments and may be relatively less influenced by salt water. The mouths of such large rivers often have numerous branches forming a delta, with extensive brackish and salt marshes and, upriver a bit, more freshwater swamps and bayous, including vast tracts of permanently flooded woodland. Where there is enough protection from the ocean or gulf waves, especially in the Florida peninsula, mangrove swamps may develop. These areas are known far and wide to bird enthusiasts as dazzling places to watch waterbirds.

WOOD STORK

In the protected coastal habitats of the Gulf of Mexico, a morning trip to a marsh or mangrove swamp might produce not only many of the species mentioned previously as nesters or migrants but also some southern "specialty" birds, such as the white ibis, white-faced ibis, long-billed curlew, roseate spoonbill, and magnificent frigatebird.

Another southern specialty sometimes present in these habitats, but more closely tied to cypress swamps and drying freshwater ponds of interior wetlands, is the stately wood stork, the only species of stork present in North America.

WHOOPING CRANE

The rarest waterbird of the Gulf and Atlantic shores is the endangered whooping crane. A small flock winters in coastal marshes at the Aransas National Wildlife Refuge in Texas.

In areas of very shallow, salty water, called salt pans, near the Gulf coast, reddish egrets may be seen chasing minnows and other prey, often in company with other herons.

22

Coastal ecosystems are fragile. Between the ceaseless and very complex interactions of freshwater and saltwater environments along the coastlines, millions of waterbirds make their living. They are able to anticipate the rhythms of the coast's ecosystems and thus can locate the optimal feeding places and times with unerring accuracy.

Many species return as migrants, nesters, or winterers to precisely the same beach or marsh where they spent the previous season —or, in some cases, where their ancestors foraged thousands of generations before.

It is a sad fact of modern life that the 20th century's population explosion in North America has made areas of coastline more and more desirable and more densely developed and populated than at any other time in history. Fragile coastal environments have been altered, with any number of con-sequences, mostly negative, for birds and other wildlife.

Bulkheads that provide a perch for gulls, terns, and cormorants may mark the former site of a lush salt marsh. Rock jetties and artificial stone islands may change the pattern of beach erosion in some places for better or for worse. They have turned out to be beneficial for some birds, particularly those

23

that require rocky habitats—purple sand-pipers, great cormorants, and eider ducks. These birds can often be found on or near such structures, well south of their "normal" New England range, sometimes even down into the Carolinas!

Likewise, dredge-spoil islands, the by-products of creating deeper channels for ship traffic and deeper harbors, marinas, and anchorages, have become havens for nesting brown pelicans, herons, ibises, and many tern species, as these artificial islands mimic the natural barrier islands and bars created by tidal activity.

But the beneficial changes are exceptional. Dunes that once protected estuaries and other interior habitats—and that comprised important habitats in their own right—have been lost to the construction of beach homes, hotels, and boardwalks, particularly in the Southeast and New Jersey and New York. Very little intact coastal habitat survives out-side protected areas; the southern maritime forest is almost extinct.

It is hoped that users of this guide will remember the fragility of coastal environments they visit, tread lightly and respect their inhabitants, and support local efforts to preserve the health of North America's coasts.

HOW TO LOOK AT A WATER-BIRD

AERIALISTS

SWIMMERS

WADING BIRDS

SHOREBIRDS

The way birds feed and their adaptations for feeding are the most important points to recognize in identifying and understanding them. For the beginner, the color and pattern of an unknown bird can be so striking that important points of shape and behavior go unnoticed. But feeding adaptations, especially bill shape, best reveal a bird's role in nature—its truest identity.

Waterbirds use one of four general strategies for catching prey. There are aerialists, swimmers, wading birds, and shorebirds. The exception is the kingfisher. Birds that use the same general strategy resemble one another, and the differences between birds that use different strategies can be recognized at a distance without binoculars.

The aerialists, such as gulls and terns, fly on long, slender wings, scanning the water and shores below in search of food. Some simply pick prey or scavenge from the surface. The magnificent frigatebird picks while in flight and seldom even gets its feathers wet. Other aerialists plunge-dive rather than pick. They search for fish swimming close to the water's surface and attack by folding their wings and plunging headfirst into the water below. The gannet plunge-dives from heights of 25 feet or more.

The swimmers, such as ducks and cormorants, search for food from the water's surface. Some dive to chase fish or feed from bottoms that can be 100 feet below the surface. Others, like geese and the ducks known as dabblers, don't dive but feed from the surface or tip up to graze on vegetation growing on shallow bottoms. The grazers also take vegetation at the water's edge. Some geese travel to nearby croplands to feed on grains and growing plants.

The swimmers have wide bodies for floating on the water; most have webbed feet. Their profile on the water is very different from that of a resting gull, and their flight is swift and direct, not at all like the slow, searching flight of the aerialists.

The wading birds and shorebirds pursue their prey on foot. The wading birds, such as herons, stalk through marshes and wetlands, often capturing prey such as fish, frogs, and crabs with a sudden thrust of a dagger-like bill. Nearly all except some elusive rails are large birds with long legs and heavy bills.

Shorebirds typically probe for small marine organisms on the mudflats, beaches, and rocks of the intertidal zone. Their bills are slender for efficient probing. The larger shorebirds and some of the smaller ones, too, have remarkably long bills (check out the curlews on p. 102).

Note that shorebirds often wade, and wading birds can be seen on mudflats and marsh edges with shorebirds. Because they both stalk prey on foot, the larger shorebirds and the wading birds have many similarities—long legs, long necks, and elongated bodies. Bill shape is a good structural mark for separating them. Also note that herons can fold their necks and often do; shorebirds can't.

In this guide, waterbirds are grouped by their four general foraging styles. Within each group, birds are listed by size, the larger birds illustrated first. Birds of similar size and shape usually have distinctive plumages, but a few species closely resemble one another and must be identified carefully.

Young birds, seen in summer and fall, often have a different plumage than adults, but each is the same size and shape as the adult. Any young bird that has a plumage confusingly different from the adult's is illustrated. Some young birds molt to adult plumage in their first fall, but many take longer. Large gulls wear distinctive immature plumage until they are three or four years old.

Most names used to describe parts of a water-bird are fairly predictable—back, crown, bill, etc. "Mantle" and "speculum" are not as obvious. Mantle refers to the back and adjoining wing areas, which are often the same color. The speculum is the bright patch on the trailing edge of a duck's wing, near the body. Many ducks, including all the dabblers, have speculums, which are useful identification marks.

HOW TO READ THE MAPS

Range maps provide a simplified picture of a species' distribution. They indicate the birds that can be expected at any locality. Birds are not evenly distributed over their ranges. They require suitable habitat and are typically scarcest at their range limits. Some birds seem scarce because they are secretive.

Many birds that live on the coast for most of the year migrate inland or to the Arctic to nest. A few species that live elsewhere are seen on our coasts only in migration. Spring migration can last until mid-June for some species. By early July a few of the earliest nesters (usually the unsuccessful ones) are already winging it south. For shorebirds, spring migration peaks in April and May; fall migration, in August and September.

MAP KEY

SUMMER OR NESTING

WINTER

ALL YEAR

MIGRATION
(spring & fall)

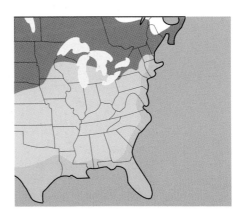

THE BIRDS

Not all ducks are called ducks—eider, teal, and scaup, for instance, are all ducks. In the list below, birds with names different from their common group name are listed in parentheses following the group name.

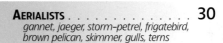

GANNET

WILSON'S STORM-PETREL

PARASITIC JAEGER

Although few of us landlubbers ever see one, Wilson's storm-petrel is thought to be one of the most abundant birds in the world.

More than two dozen species of birds fly over Atlantic and Gulf waters, feeding on prey near the surface. Usually they come ashore only in remote areas and then only to nest, but with good binoculars, the gannet, parasitic jaeger, and Wilson's storm-petrel can sometimes be seen and identified from shore.

Gannets are at their northern nesting colonies in summer. In winter, flocks can sometimes be seen fishing near the horizon off many points on the eastern seaboard. They plunge-dive for fish and feed singly as well as in groups. Large migrating flocks gather in early spring and late fall. The **gannet's** plumage and shape (pointed at both ends) are both distinctive.

Jaegers are muscular, predatory cousins of gulls. They fly solo and pirate the catch of others. Some **parasitic jaegers** migrate near shore in spring and fall. Plumage varies considerably. The white flash in the wing is a good field mark. The pointed tail streamers are absent in young birds and can be missing in adults.

Wilson's storm-petrel is small (only 7 inches long) and has a white rump. It is a summer visitor that is occasionally seen from beaches and sometimes occurs singly or in small groups in bays and outer harbors. It flies swallow-like and patters on the water when feeding.

young

Gannet

Parasitic Jaeger

Wilson's
Storm-petrel

dark form

young

pale form

FRIGATEBIRD AND PELICAN

MAGNIFICENT FRIGATEBIRD

BROWN PELICAN

Frigatebirds rarely rest on the water like other waterbirds. Their plumage is not waterproof and becomes soaked. If this happens, their long, slender wings, perfect for soaring, can't generate enough lift for them to become airborne.

Both pelicans and frigatebirds have such distinctive shapes that they can be recognized even when seen as specks in the distance. Frigatebirds glide and soar singly or in small groups. The male **magnificent frigatebird** is glossy black and has an inflatable red throat pouch. The female is flat black and has a white breast. Young birds are colored like females, but their heads as well as their breasts are white.

The magnificent frigatebird is a tropical bird, numerous only in the Gulf of Mexico. It uses its long bill to snatch fish near the water's surface. It is also a pirate, harassing gulls and terns into giving up their catch.

The brown pelican makes dramatic plunge-dives amid schools of fish, using its huge bill and pouch to scoop them up. (White pelicans, p. 52, are swimmers, not plunge-divers.) Decimated in the 1960s by pesticides, brown pelicans are now numerous on the Atlantic, often looking for handouts at piers and marinas. They are becoming common on the Gulf.

In winter, the **brown pelican** has a golden head and white neck. The head fades to white in summer, and the hind neck becomes reddish brown. Young birds have a dark head and neck.

White Pelican
p. 52

♂

Magnificent
Frigatebird

Brown
Pelican

winter

summer

1st year

BLACK SKIMMER

GREAT BLACK-BACKED GULL

Lesser black-backed gulls are rare but increasing in winter along the Atlantic coast and the Gulf. They are smaller than the great black-backed, slightly smaller even than the herring gull (p. 38). The mantle is usually dark gray (not black), the legs are yellow, and the hind neck is heavily streaked in winter.

Bill shape reveals a lot about a bird. Bills are the tools with which birds forage, and in the case of the black skimmer, the tool is highly specialized. The long, thin lower mandible slices the water like a knife as the skimmer flies just above the surface. When the lower mandible contacts prey, the shorter upper mandible snaps shut, capturing it.

When not fishing, skimmers often gather on sandbars. Like gulls and terns, they stand facing into the wind. The bill color and short upper mandible of the **black skimmer** can be seen at a moderate distance. Even at long distances, the black upperparts of adults can be distinguished. The great black-backed gull is the only similar bird with a black mantle.

Look for skimmers feeding on quiet lagoons and open salt marshes, often at night. Good light is not important, as they feed by touch, but smooth water is critical.

Not only is the **great black-backed gull** the only gull with a black mantle, but it is the largest gull on the beach, actually the largest in the world! It is often seen singly among other gulls, and it stands out. Seen flying overhead, it is not as distinctive, but note how the black on the underwing extends in a bar from the black outer wing to the body.

34

winter

young

Black Skimmer

summer

Great Black-backed
Gull

GULLS

ICELAND GULL

GLAUCOUS GULL

The brownish gulls that predominate on most beaches are young birds. Their identification is discussed on p. 42.

There are two large adult gulls with pale gray mantles and white, or nearly white, wing tips. The glaucous gull is the larger; the Iceland gull is smaller and usually shows some pale gray in the wing tips, although this probably won't be seen without binoculars. The heads, necks, and breasts of both species are usually streaked with gray or tan in winter, when they visit the coasts of the north and middle Atlantic states. Neither gull is numerous on US coasts, and they are progressively scarcer south of New England.

Size differences are difficult to judge unless the two species are standing side by side. The best clinching mark without binoculars is the distance the folded wing on a standing bird extends beyond the tail. The wings of the **glaucous gull** barely extend beyond the tail (less than the length of the bill); those of the **Iceland gull** extend more than its bill length.

There are usually obvious differences in head and bill shape of the two species as well. The glaucous gull has a sloping forehead and a heavy bill more than half the length of the head. The Iceland has a smaller, rounder head and a shorter, more slender bill that is often greenish yellow. The bill of the glaucous gull is never greenish.

Iceland

glaucous

summer **Iceland Gull** winter

Iceland

glaucous

summer

winter **Glaucous Gull**

HERRING GULL

RING-BILLED GULL

The red spot on the bill seen on many adult gulls is thought to be a pecking target for nestlings demanding food.

Young herring gulls (p. 42) can also show a dark ring on their bills. Young gulls are brownish and have a dark band on the tail.

nlike the pale-backed gulls in the preceding illustration, adult herring and ring-billed gulls show black in their wing tips. The black is easily seen at a distance whether the bird is flying or standing.

In winter, herring and ring-billed gulls are two of the most abundant gulls on the shores and salt marshes of the Gulf and Atlantic, spilling over into nearby communities and landfills. Only the laughing gull (p. 40) is as common.

Most adult ring-bills withdraw from coasts in the spring to nest in the interior, and they don't return until fall. But some individuals don't nest; they remain at the shore throughout the summer. The same is true of adult herring gulls, which mostly desert the south Atlantic and Gulf shores in summer; a few remain. North of the Carolina coast, herring gulls are abundant throughout the year.

A **herring gull** is almost half again the size of a **ring-billed gull.** (The body of the herring gull is somewhat foreshortened in the illustration.) The size difference is noticeable even at a distance when the birds are seen together, as they often are. At closer range, the distinctive bill markings are noticeable. Leg color is distinctive as well: yellow or greenish yellow in the ring-bill, pink or fleshy in the herring gull.

summer

Herring Gull

winter

herring

ring-billed

herring

Ring-billed Gull

summer

winter

BONAPARTE'S GULL

LAUGHING GULL

Franklin's gulls nest inland and are seen in migration over the coasts of Texas and Louisiana in spring and fall. They most closely resemble the laughing gull but are smaller and have both white and black markings on their wing tips.

The laughing gull and Bonaparte's gull are the two smallest gulls commonly seen on Atlantic and Gulf shores. In spring and early summer, adults have distinctive black hoods; some show a delicate pink blush on their white breasts. By late summer, the heads begin turning white with a few gray markings.

The black hood and red bill are good marks for adult **laughing gulls** in summer. Molting birds and yearlings show a partially complete hood. By fall, the head is nearly white and the bill has turned dark. Another reliable mark is the namesake call.

The laughing gull is abundant in spring and summer. It has adapted well to people and is as comfortable as a ring-billed gull (p. 38) scavenging from the parking lot of a coastal fast-food franchise. Most laughing gulls migrate south in fall, but some overwinter as far north as Chesapeake Bay.

Bonaparte's gulls are absent from shores in the summer—except for an occasional straggler. They leave in spring wearing black hoods and return in fall with just a dark smudge on the side of the head. **Bonaparte's gull** has a slender black bill, much finer than that of the laughing gull. In flight, the triangle of white at the tip of the wings is distinctive.

summer

winter

Bonaparte's

summer

winter

laughing

Bonaparte's

laughing

Laughing Gull

Bonaparte's
Gull

YOUNG GULLS

When everything else on the beach has been identified, try your hand at the young brown gulls. All the brownish gulls with a dark band on their tails are young birds.

It takes four years in the larger species for a young gull to attain the smooth gray-and-white plumage of an adult. Ring-billed and laughing gulls mature in three years; Bonaparte's in just two. At each molt (twice a year), their appearance changes. The youngest birds, in their first-winter plumage, are the darkest and have dark eyes. The plumage color lightens each spring and fall until adult plumage is achieved.

Young birds are the same size as adults, and size is a good clue in a mixed flock. Identify the adults, then match the young gulls with them by size when possible. Next, check the bill shape. Bill shape is the same in young birds as in adults, although size can vary individually.

Bill and plumage markings are the final points. Note that the first-winter ring-billed has a black-tipped bill; the ring forms by the second winter when the plumage is nearly as pale as the adult's. In the first-year herring gull, the black tip of the bill blends to a pale base. In its second year, the herring gull's bill can show a ring similar to that on a ring-billed gull, but the herring gull is darker, especially on the tail.

Typically there will be as many or more young gulls (one to three years old) on a beach as there are mature gulls, which can live 20 years or more. And perhaps half the young birds will be in their first year. The proportions of the age groups reveal the story of early mortality in gulls.

42

Bonaparte's Gull

Laughing Gull

Ring-billed Gull

Iceland Gull

Great Black-backed Gull

Glaucous Gull

3rd winter

2nd winter

Herring Gull

ALL STANDING BIRDS 1ST WINTER

TERNS

ROYAL TERN

CASPIAN TERN

Young terns resemble winter adults but have contrasting flecking or barring on their mantles. In many species, the young have dusky tail tips and wing patches. Young Caspians often have red legs.

One- and two-year-old terns usually remain on the wintering grounds, but some are seen and suggest worn winter adults.

Terns look different than gulls, although the two are closely related. Terns are more slender and streamlined; most have pointed bills, long pointed wings, and forked tails. Although the Caspian and royal terns are gull-sized, most terns are smaller than gulls. The black cap is another good mark for a tern; most wear them throughout the summer.

Terns behave differently than gulls too. They don't interrupt their wing beats to glide on the shore breeze, as gulls often do. A tern strokes continuously, often cruising 10 or 20 feet above the water with its bill pointed down as it scans for small fish. Terns typically hover over suspected prey, then plunge headfirst to capture it, something gulls rarely do.

Its bulky body and heavy red bill distinguish the **Caspian tern** in all seasons. Even seen flying at a distance, it can be separated from the royal tern by the large dark patch on the underside of the wing. The black cap is streaked with white in winter.

The **royal tern** has a more slender and more orange bill, and it also has a white forehead most of the year. Only for a few weeks during nesting season (typically in spring) does it wear a full black cap. The rest of the year, the black nape looks like a balding man's fringe.

44

royal

breeding

nonbreeding

Caspian

summer

winter

royal

Caspian

breeding

young

Royal
Tern

young

Caspian
Tern

summer

COMMON TERN

FORSTER'S TERN

Roseate terns nest in very small numbers from the Canadian Maritimes to Long Island, NY. A second, small population nests in the Florida Keys.

The roseate tern has a longer tail than even Forster's. The bill is nearly all black (with some red at the base), and the mantle is so pale that it does not contrast with the white rump or tail.

Smaller than the Caspian and royal terns shown on the previous page, Forster's and common terns also sport black tips on their red or orange bills in summer. At least the adults do. A young bird in summer looks similar to the winter adult; both have all-black bills and may be confused with the black-billed terns in the next illustration.

In winter, only Forster's tern is present in the US; note the distinctive eye patch and the plain shoulder (the common tern has a dark shoulder bar in fall and winter). In summer, Forster's and common terns can be difficult to separate, even with binoculars.

One of the first clues in summer is habitat. **Forster's** prefers marshes, where it preys on large flying insects more often than fish. The **common tern** prefers plunging for fish near shore. However, both species are comfortable behaving like the other. Bill color is also helpful but not a certain clue. The bill is typically more orange in Forster's. In flight, the outer surface of the upper wing is the best mark. It is paler (frosted looking, some say) than the mantle in Forster's; a small, dark wedge is visible in the common. When the bird is standing, Forster's long forked tail is a useful mark, extending beyond the folded wing tip. The common's tail does not reach the wing tips.

common

Forster's

summer

summer

winter

winter

common
(late summer)

Forster's

summer

Common Tern

young

winter

young

summer

**Forster's
Tern**

winter

TERNS

SANDWICH TERN

GULL-BILLED TERN

Since the 1970s, tern nesting colonies have come under increasing pressure from predatory herring gulls and great black-backed gulls. Numbers of the two gulls are increasing at the expense of terns.

Sandwich and gull-billed terns are slightly larger than the common and Forster's terns shown on the preceding page. However, sandwich and gull-billed terns are scarcer and never show orange or red in their bills.

The sandwich tern is often seen fishing out over the breakers, where it is not likely to be identified without binoculars. When not fishing, it often associates with royal terns (p. 44) on sandbars and beaches. Like the royal tern, **sandwich terns** show full black caps only briefly during nesting season, usually in spring. The rest of the year they have a black fringe on the hind crown, again like the royal tern. Their best mark is the long, slender black bill with a yellow tip.

The bill is the best mark for the **gull-billed tern** too. It is shaped more like a gull's bill than a tern's. In fact, this tern is intermediate to a gull and a tern in many ways. It is stocky for a tern, and its wings are a bit wider than those of other terns, more gull-like. Its tail is short and only shallowly forked.

Gull-billed terns don't often plunge-dive for fish. They prefer catching large insects in mid-air over marshes and fields. They were once numerous on Atlantic marshes but never recovered from their slaughter for use as fashion ornaments in the late nineteenth century.

48

breeding

non-breeding   sandwich

summer

winter

gull-billed

sandwich

gull-billed

Sandwich Tern

young

young   summer

Gull-billed Tern

TERNS

BLACK TERN

Since the 1960s, the black tern has been seriously declining, especially in the East. Flocks of several hundred migrating birds once were fairly commonplace. Now such a flock is rare.

The cause of the decline is uncertain, but damage to the nesting habitat is suspected.

The least and black terns are the smallest and most endangered of the terns. Least terns are summer visitors that prefer to nest on sand beaches or shell banks above the high water line. They have been displaced from most such sites by people. Many least terns now attempt to nest on a variety of substitute sites, including gravel rooftops, sand and gravel pits, even parking lots. The most successful substitutes have been islands of dredge-spoil in rivers and bays.

The least tern prefers fishing in shallow water. When it sights a fish, it often hovers above it before plunging. Least terns are seen singly or in small groups, just offshore from ocean beaches and in bays and inlets. The small size is one good mark for the **least tern;** the yellow bill with black tip is the clincher. Also note the patch of white on the forehead.

Black terns nest in the interior and winter south of the US, but flocks migrate along the shore and offshore, especially in August and September. Nonbreeders gather along the Gulf coast in summer. Adult **black terns** are obvious in breeding plumage. Nonbreeders, probably yearlings, are white below, like young birds and winter adults. In fall migration, molting birds with patchy underparts can be seen.

50

summer

least

black

winter

least

black

summer

fall (molting)

young

young

summer

summer

Least Tern

Black Tern

PELICAN AND SWANS

WHITE PELICAN

MUTE SWAN

TUNDRA SWAN

In fall and winter, white pelicans fish in the warm waters of the Gulf coast. They don't patrol the shoreline and plunge-dive for fish like brown pelicans—or hang out at piers, either. White pelicans capture fish while swimming in inlets, bays, and similar protected coastal shallows. They simply use their bills like nets to scoop up small schooling fish.

It's hard to sneak up on prey when you're the size of a white pelican. The pelicans solve that problem by fishing together. Through coordinated movements, they herd small schooling fish toward each other or into shore.

One does not need binoculars to identify a **white pelican.** Before nesting, a plate-like protrusion grows on the ridge of the bill.

The **mute swan** is the familiar swan that decorates parks and estates, swimming with its wings flared and neck gracefully curved. Originally from Europe, it has established itself in the wild and now winters in protected coastal waters from New Hampshire to North Carolina.

Don't confuse **tundra swans** with mute swans. The head and bill, among other features, are distinctly different. Tundra swans aren't saltwater birds but can be seen at brackish river mouths and freshwater ponds or marshes near the coast in winter.

By 1993, there were an estimated 10,000 mute swans along the Atlantic coast. They have become aggressive pests in some areas, prompting efforts to control their numbers.

Brown Pelican
p. 32

Mute Swan

Tundra Swan

tundra swan

White Pelican

GEESE

WHITE-FRONTED GOOSE

SNOW GOOSE

Look for a few Ross' geese in any large flock of snow geese seen on the Texas or Louisiana coast.

Ross' goose looks like a small white-form snow goose but has a stubbier bill, lacks the "grinning patch," and often shows a dull purplish area at the base of the bill.

One snow goose race, the greater snow goose, winters in large flocks on the Atlantic coast, mostly near Chesapeake Bay. They often feed in grass and grain fields but prefer shallow coastal bays and marshes at night for roosting.

A second snow goose population, the lesser snow goose, winters primarily in the western Gulf. The difference in size of lesser and greater snow geese is not noticeable, but flocks of lesser snow geese include many of a dark form known as blue geese (illustrated in flight). The dark form is rare in flocks of greater snow geese. Both forms of the **snow goose** can be identified by the white head. Also note the dark "lips" or "grinning patch" where the cutting edges of the bill meet.

The white-fronted goose also winters along the western Gulf coast. It grazes on marsh vegetation as well as grasses and grains from nearby fields. The name refers to the small white band above the bill. Another mark for the adult **white-fronted goose** is the dark speckled belly. Legs are usually orange; the bill is usually pink, but these colors vary. Flocks fly in Vs and give a high-pitched, two-noted, "laughing" call. Escaped domestic gray geese can be mistaken for the white-fronted goose.

domestic goose

young

White-fronted Goose

white-fronted

blue goose form of snow goose

Snow Goose

young

GEESE

BRANT

CANADA GOOSE

Most of the Canada geese seen along the Atlantic coast are the same size, but occasionally a small bird can be found.

Few people need an introduction to the **Canada goose.** The black stocking–like head and neck and the white chin strap are familiar across the continent. Flying flocks are recognized by the V-formation flight and resounding honks. There are many races, including duck-sized "cackling geese" in the West and "giant" ones in the Midwest.

Canada geese are primarily grazers. Along the Atlantic coast, some live on tidal flats, taking mollusks and marine life, but most feed on marsh grasses and other vegetation. Golf courses and similar grassy areas attract flocks that now stay year-round. In some areas, Canada geese have become pests.

Brant are grazers also. In winter, they specialize in eelgrass, which grows in shallow salt water, and are seen only occasionally on lawns. Brant begin to arrive along the Atlantic coast by mid-October and are often seen in small flocks. In February and March, they concentrate in large flocks in the mid-Atlantic and begin moving north. The last birds leave in May.

Brant are geese that are barely larger than a mallard. On the water, they look dark overall until they tip up to feed and display their bright, white rears. At close range, a stylish white design can be seen on the neck of adults.

Brant

brant

Canada

Canada Goose

large race
with white neck ring

giant race

small race:
cackling goose

LOONS

RED-THROATED LOON

COMMON LOON

Loons propel themselves underwater by their webbed feet, as do the cormorants (p. 60) and the grebes (p. 82).

The alcids (p. 62), on the other hand, use their feet as rudders and "fly" underwater with their wings.

Loons spend almost their entire lives on the water, diving for fish. They come ashore to nest, usually just a few feet from the water's edge on a tiny islet or peninsula. They nest on fresh water, but the great majority migrate to seacoasts for the winter. Most stay near shore or in protected deep-water bays and inlets. They usually feed separately, but common loons gather in flocks at night.

Loons usually sit low in the water instead of bobbing on top like some ducks. Because they dive for fish, loons can't be lighter than water or they couldn't submerge efficiently. They float on the surface by filling internal air sacs and by capturing air in their feathers.

Both common and red-throated loons are widespread and fairly numerous. In summer plumage, the neck and head of the two are quite different. However, the more commonly seen winter plumages resemble each other. Note the heavy bill of the **common loon** and the slender, uptilted bill of the **red-throated.** The pattern of dark and white on the side of the head and neck is also distinctive for each species. On the red-throated, the white foreneck blends to the dark hindneck smoothly and in a graceful line. On the common loon, white meets dark in a jagged line on the lower neck, like pieces of a puzzle.

Red-throated Loon

winter

summer

common

red-throated

young

winter

summer

Common Loon

CORMORANTS

DOUBLE-CRESTED
CORMORANT

GREAT
CORMORANT

Anhingas resemble cormorants but are freshwater birds, rare in salt or brackish waters. The anhinga's head and neck are more slender, and its bill is sharply pointed.

The neotropic cormorant is found on the Louisiana and Texas coasts. It is smaller than the double-crested and has a distinctively long tail for a cormorant.

A large bird seen standing on a piling with its wings spread is probably a cormorant. The heavy body, short tail, and long, slender neck and head give the cormorant a distinctive look. Anhingas (see sidebar) also spread their wings in the sun, and some others, including pelicans, do so occasionally.

Cormorants dive for fish and spread their wings in the sun to dry their plumage. The feathers on most diving birds are structured so that they are waterproof, but the outer portion of the cormorant's plumage is wetable. An inner layer is waterproof and helps keep the bird warm in cold water.

The **double-crested** is the most numerous and widespread cormorant. In most places, it is the only cormorant to be seen in summer. When not in the water, it is easily seen resting on various shoreline perches. The orange or yellow throat is the clinching mark. In flight, cormorants kink their necks distinctively.

In summer, the **great cormorant** is found only in the Canadian Maritimes. In winter, it visits coasts as far south as South Carolina. Winter adults lack the white flank patch illustrated but show the distinctive white throat band. Young birds have white bellies and dark breasts. The pattern is reversed in young double-cresteds.

Double-crested Cormorant

young

double-crested

great

Great Cormorant

young

BLACK GUILLEMOT

RAZORBILL

Nesting colonies of the Atlantic puffin are being restored on islands off the coast of Maine.

In summer, the Atlantic puffin has black-and-white plumage and a brightly colored, blade-like bill nearly as large as its head.

Both the razorbill and black guillemot are alcids, oceanic birds that come ashore only to nest in remote areas. Unlike the oceanic aerialists (p. 30), alcids swim on the water's surface and catch their prey (mostly fish) by diving and giving chase.

Black guillemots *(GILL-la-mots)* and razorbills are the two alcids most likely to be seen off the Atlantic coast of the US. (Binoculars or a telescope is usually necessary.) They come south in cold winter waters. Razorbills are fairly numerous off New England, often in small groups. In some years, they venture as far south as Cape Hatteras, NC. Black guillemots occur south to Massachussets.

Seen at close range, the bill is the **razorbill's** best mark. The black-and-white plumage pattern (sometimes noted in flight near the horizon) is a helpful mark but not a sure one unless seen closely; it resembles that of several other alcids and the oldsquaw (p. 76).

Black guillemots are mostly white in winter, but they retain their distinctive black wings with large white wing patches throughout the year. Some birds hold most of their summer black plumage well into winter. Black guillemots are usually seen singly or in small groups well beyond the breakers.

62

winter

summer

guillemot

Black Guillemot

razorbill

Razorbill

summer

young

winter

BLACK DUCK

MOTTLED DUCK

MALLARD

The brightly colored wing patch is known as the speculum and is a useful mark. It is bright blue with white borders in the mallard, purple in the black duck, and usually greenish in the mottled duck.

Mallards prefer fresh water but also live in shallow protected salt water along the coast. They won't be seen on deep water; they are not diving ducks but dabblers—ducks that tip up to feed on bottom vegetation.

Nothing looks like a male **mallard,** although the male shoveler (p. 68) has a green head. Many ducks, however, resemble the mottled-brown female mallard. Her best marks are her bill, tail, and feather pattern. The bill is orange with a black saddle mark on top, the tail shows white, and the body feathers are truly mottled.

On Atlantic coast marshes, black ducks may outnumber mallards, but few people notice. **Black ducks** resemble female mallards but are darker (male darkest). The easiest mark is the dark tail. The male's bill is yellow; the female's, yellow-green with some black flecking. Note that the body feathers have buff edges but no interior mottling. Black ducks hybridize with mallards; intermediates are common.

Mottled ducks are residents of the Gulf coast and Florida; mallards are winter visitors. The **mottled duck** has a dark tail and yellow bill (dark flecking on the female's). Note the contrast of the dark body with the pale unstreaked throat and cheek. Mottled ducks hybridize with feral mallards, producing intermediates.

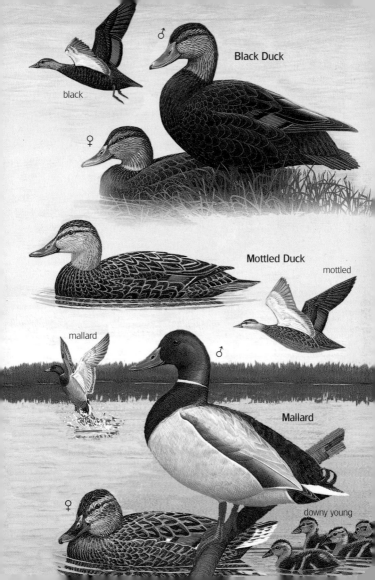

black

♂

Black Duck

♀

Mottled Duck

mottled

mallard

♂

Mallard

♀

downy young

DUCKS

GADWALL

PINTAIL

AMERICAN
WIGEON

Rarely in a flock of
American wigeons it is
possible to see a
Eurasian wigeon. The
male Eurasian wigeon
has a red-brown head
and a buff crown; its
sides are gray. Females
are very much like
American wigeons.

Gadwalls, pintails, and wigeons are dabblers like mallards. A few gadwalls and wigeons nest along the Atlantic in summer, but they and the pintail are primarily winter visitors on the Gulf and Atlantic coasts. Most settle on freshwater marsh or brackish inlets, but some are found on saltwater bays and marshes.

Gadwalls are most common in winter on the Texas and Louisiana coast. They are usually seen in small flocks, often with pintails. The male **gadwall** is a finely detailed gray-brown. Look for the black rear end and the contrast of the brown head with the gray body. The female suggests a female mallard, but note the white belly and the gray bill with orange edges. Both sexes have a distinctive white speculum.

Pintails are numerous but unevenly distributed along the coasts in winter. It would be hard to mistake a male. Females resemble other brown females. The white belly is a useful mark, but the longish bill, rounded head, and long, slender neck are the best marks. Head and bill profiles are a reliable mark for most ducks.

Note the short bill of the **American wigeon.** Male wigeons are bright with a white or creamy forehead; females, brown with a grayish head. The green speculum and white shoulder patch (grayish in females) are good marks in flight..

gadwall

wigeon

Gadwall

♀ ♂

Pintail

♂ ♀

American Wigeon

♂ ♀

SHOVELER

BLUE-WINGED
TEAL

GREEN-WINGED
TEAL

A few cinnamon teal
migrate and winter on
the lower Texas coast.
Males are largely
cinnamon colored;
females resemble
female blue-wings,
but have duller faces
and larger bills.

Teal are the smallest dabbling ducks. They and the shoveler are closely related, and all can be found in shallow coastal marshes and protected bays and inlets in winter.

The shoveler is scarce on the Atlantic coast in winter, more common on the Texas and Louisiana coasts, often in small flocks. The outsized bill and long, sloping forehead give the **shoveler,** male and female, a very special look. The bill is specialized for straining tiny aquatic animals from the water, and the bird is often seen swimming low in the water with its bill, even its head, submerged. In flight, shovelers resemble blue-winged teal, with green speculums and blue wing patches.

Like most dabbling ducks, the male **green-winged** and **blue-winged teal** are bright and distinctive. Females are much alike when seen swimming—small and mottled brown, with dark bills. The green-winged teal has the smallest bill, and it lacks the bright blue forewing patch that the blue-winged teal shows in flight.

Green-winged teal are more common in winter than the blue-winged. Most blue-winged teal winter south of the US. They don't become numerous until migrants appear on the Texas and Louisiana coasts in spring.

Shoveler

1st winter ♂

♀

♂

Blue-winged Teal

♂

♀

♂

♀

Green-winged Teal

♂

DUCKS

RING-NECKED
DUCK

LESSER SCAUP

GREATER SCAUP

So why is it called
the ring-necked duck
when the ring is on
the bill? Because,
with the bird in hand,
a faint purple-brown
collar can be seen.
The name harkens
back to the days
when bird-watching
was done with a gun.

Scaup and ring-necked ducks dive to feed on bottom vegetation and aquatic life such as mussels and barnacles. They are winter visitors except in the Northeast, where some ring-necked ducks nest on coastal fresh water.

Ring-necked ducks are scarce on salt water even in winter, but they do accept brackish water. Like scaup, they usually feed in shallow water, although they can dive 40 feet deep. In very shallow water, they tip up like dabblers.

The white bill-ring is a good mark for the **ring-necked duck.** At a distance, the white sides and black back are sufficient for the male. Scaup have gray backs. In the female, note the thin white eye-ring and pale line behind the eye.

Scaup are difficult to separate. Females also closely resemble female ring-necks and red-heads (p. 72). The **lesser scaup** has a slightly smaller bill and a more peaked head; the **greater scaup's** crown is more rounded. Male greater scaups have paler backs; females can show a pale spot on the side of the head in fall and winter not seen in most lesser scaup. In flight, both scaup show a white band on the trailing edge of the upperwing. On the lesser scaup the band turns gray on the outer wing.

Large flocks ("rafts") of scaup often form in bays and nearshore ocean waters.

Ring-necked Duck

♂ ♀

ring-
necked

Lesser Scaup

♂ ♀

lesser

greater

Greater Scaup

♀ ♂

REDHEAD

CANVASBACK

RUDDY DUCK

Most diving ducks propel themselves underwater with webbed feet. For efficient diving, legs are placed well back on the body, so far back that some, like the ruddy duck, struggle to walk on land.

Canvasbacks, redheads, and ruddy ducks are divers that feed primarily on bottom vegetation. All are winter visitors to the Atlantic and Gulf coasts, where they flock in protected bays and marshes. A flock of canvasbacks or redheads can number in the hundreds.

Like the redhead, the male canvasback has a black breast and a chestnut head and neck, but its back and sides are nearly white compared to the gray-bodied redhead. Best mark for the **canvasback**—especially the female—is the long, slightly dished bill and forehead.

Redheads have a fairly steep forehead and a rounded head. The bill is average sized and tipped with black. Female redheads are very much like the female scaup shown on the previous page; they are closely related. Female redheads are a tawnier brown than scaup and don't show white at the base of the bill, although the area near the bill may be pale.

Ruddy ducks usually keep to themselves in small, loose groups instead of flocking with other species. Their stiff tails, often cocked at a 45-degree angle, give **ruddy ducks** an unusual look. The bright blue bill of the male is an easy mark in summer; the white cheeks are good marks year-round. Females have gray cheeks divided by a dark line.

72

redhead

canvasback

♀

♂

Redhead

♀

♂

Canvasback

Ruddy Duck

summer ♂

winter ♂

♀

DUCKS

KING EIDER

COMMON EIDER

The fine, insulating down that protects the common eider in temperatures down to -50°F is prized by mankind for use in clothing and bedding. Collecting it from the nests of common eiders is a small industry in Iceland.

Eiders "fly" underwater with their wings. Common eiders can burst from under the water and into the air in full flight.

Eiders are hardy diving ducks of cold ocean waters. Their luxurious plumage protects them in temperatures well below freezing. Common eiders range as far south as North Carolina in winter. King eiders are rare south of Maryland.

Mussels are the favorite food of both eiders, but they also eat crabs, sea urchins, starfish, and more. They swallow shellfish whole, grinding the shell in their gizzards. Feeding takes place at low tide and is often near shore over shellfish beds. At night, eiders usually gather in large flocks, often out of sight of land.

An eider's bill extends in a shield well up the forehead, protecting the bird from cuts while feeding. The male **king eider's** shield is awesome. The male **common eider's** shield isn't as flashy, but the bird's shape and plumage are identifiable from afar. Young male eiders are darker than adults but distinctive.

Female eiders are brown, but at close range, the feather patterns can be seen to be quite different. Heads and bills are different too. The female king eider's head is rounder; her bill, shorter. And the feathering on her forehead comes much farther down the bill. The female common eider has a profile much like that of the canvasback (see preceding page).

74

1st winter ♂

♀ ♂

King Eider

king

common

Common Eider

1st winter ♂

♀ ♂

OLDSQUAW

BUFFLEHEAD

**COMMON
GOLDENEYE**

A few Barrow's gold-
eneyes winter south
to Cape Cod. Barrow's
has a stubbier bill
than the common
goldeneye and a much
steeper forehead.
Males show a white
crescent on the face
instead of a white dot.

Buffleheads, goldeneyes, and oldsquaws are hardy ducks that live on coastal bays, rivers, inlets, and harbors in winter. They are sometimes seen over shellfish beds in the open ocean beyond the breakers but generally prefer protected waters. All dive for shellfish and small amounts of vegetation.

Flocks of **oldsquaws** are very noisy and active on the water. They winter off coasts south to North Carolina. Plumages vary, but note the short bill and small head with a fairly steep forehead. Males have long tails.

The bufflehead is the smallest diving duck. The largest winter concentration is from New Jersey to North Carolina. **Buffleheads** are often seen singly or in small groups and are quite active. Note the large puffy head, steep forehead, and short bill. Males have a large white head patch; females, a small white cheek patch.

The common goldeneye is most numerous from Chesapeake Bay northward in winter. It is known as the whistler or whistling duck for the sound made by its wings in flight. The white spot on the face of the male **common goldeneye** is a sure mark; sometimes a green gloss can be seen on the black head. The female has a rusty brown head and a narrow white collar; the yellow near the bill tip can be absent.

spring ♂ ♀

Oldsquaw

♂ winter ♀

oldsquaw

bufflehead

goldeneye

♀ ♂

Bufflehead

♀ ♂

Common Goldeneye

DUCKS

BLACK SCOTER

SURF SCOTER

WHITE-WINGED
SCOTER

In winter, a few harlequin ducks feed in turbulent surf along rocky coasts south to Virginia. The male has clownish white spots and streaks on its dark head and body. Females have small white facial spots.

Scoters are diving ducks seen in bays and off the open shoreline along the Atlantic coast in winter. A few winter off the Gulf coast. They often raft together in large numbers over shellfish beds. The concentrations of each species vary along the coast, with the white-winged being the least numerous to the south.

Scoters are dark. The coot (p. 80) is also dark, and other swimmers can appear dark in poor light. The male **black scoter** is the darkest. It has a distinctive orange bulb on its bill; females are browner and have a large whitish cheek patch. In flight, black scoters can be separated from surf scoters by the silvery patch on their underwings. Scoters fly close to the water, often in long strings.

Male **surf scoters** have the most distinctive head markings. The white spots are less pronounced on the head of the female but are still useful identification marks. The head and bill shape is a good mark as well.

On the water, the wing patch of the **white-winged scoter** is often hidden. However, the white around the eye of the adult male can be seen at a distance. Note the difference in head shape of the white-winged and black scoters and how far the feathering extends down the bill of the white-winged.

78

Black Scoter

♂ ♀

black

surf

Surf Scoter

♂ ♀

white-winged

White-winged Scoter

♂ ♀

COOT AND MERGANSER

COOT

RED-BREASTED MERGANSER

Hooded mergansers are freshwater birds sometimes found on coasts in winter. They have large crests: black and white in the male, reddish and smaller in the female.

The moorhen resembles the coot but has a thin white stripe on its side and a yellow-tipped red bill that extends onto the forehead as a shield. It sometimes ventures into brackish marshes.

The red-breasted merganser is the only merganser commonly seen on salt water in winter. The hooded merganser (see sidebar) is a freshwater bird occasionally seen on brackish river mouths and inlets. Red-breasted mergansers are numerous, both off beaches and in protected bays and harbors. They can be tame and attend fishing piers with cormorants (p. 60) and brown pelicans (p. 32).

Mergansers are divers, but unlike the diving ducks (pp. 70-79), the red-breasted merganser pursues fish primarily instead of shellfish or vegetation. Its bill has serrations for holding the slippery prey. The shaggy crest and white collar distinguish the male **red-breasted merganser** from other mergansers. On females, note that the rusty head and upper neck blends smoothly to gray below. (On female common mergansers, a freshwater bird, the meeting line is sharp.)

Coots are more closely related to rails (p. 96) than to ducks. Nevertheless, they swim like a duck and associate with ducks. On coasts in winter, they range from brackish marshes to protected bays. They feed from the surface and by diving, taking whatever they can catch, and they often graze on dry land. The **coot** is a dark bird like the scoters (p. 78) but has a chicken-like ivory bill.

Coot

young

downy young

Red-breasted Merganser

♀   ♂   young molting ♂

GREBES

PIED-BILLED
GREBE

HORNED
GREBE

RED-NECKED
GREBE

The eared grebe is a scarce winter resident along the western Gulf coast. It resembles the horned grebe in winter but has a thin, slightly upturned bill and a duskier cheek and neck.

rebes look something like small ducks, but the families are not closely related. Grebes are almost always seen on the water, as they rarely come ashore. Nests are built in marsh vegetation. They seldom fly except in migration, and then usually at night. When startled, they rapidly dive. Hell-diver is one of their common names. They dive for food—small fish, tiny shellfish, aquatic insects—and also pick morsels from the water's surface.

The pied-billed grebe is primarily a freshwater bird, but some are found in winter on brackish and salt marshes and in protected bays. It is often seen alone, and unlike other grebes, it sometimes keeps its head above water after submerging. The stubby, chicken-like bill is a distinctive mark for the **pied-billed grebe.** Its plumage is plain and brownish in winter.

Horned grebes and red-necked grebes are the most common saltwater grebes. They winter on coasts both in protected bays and beyond the breakers. Both are usually seen solo or in small groups. The **horned grebe** is a smaller bird than the **red-necked grebe** and has a shorter, more slender bill. Winter plumages of both species are similar, but the white on the horned grebe is more prevalent and extends down the neck to the water line.

82

summer

downy young

winter

Pied-billed Grebe

winter

summer

Horned Grebe

Red-necked Grebe

young

summer

winter

STORK AND SPOONBILL

WOOD STORK

ROSEATE SPOONBILL

Whooping cranes winter on the coastal marshes of Texas, most at Aransas NWR. Like the wood stork, they are white with black wing tips, but they stand nearly four feet tall and adults have red facial skin instead of black.

With considerable management, their numbers are slowly increasing.

Given a reasonable look, both the **wood stork** and **roseate spoonbill** are easy to identify. Both species are usually seen in small, loose flocks in very shallow protected waters.

The wood stork is the only stork native to North America, and since 1984 it has been on the US Fish & Wildlife Service's endangered species list. For years its numbers decreased, but it appears to have stabilized in the 1990s. Loss of foraging habitat is the big problem.

Wood storks forage by touch. They literally bump into prey (fish and other aquatic animals) by dragging their half-open bills along shallow bottoms. It is a foraging method that works best when prey is concentrated. In the winter dry season in the Southeast, prey normally becomes concentrated as swamps dry up. However, the destruction of wetlands and the regulation of drainage in the swamps that remain deprive the wood stork of the concentrated prey that it needs to nest and raise young successfully.

Spoonbills also feed by touch. Their remarkable bills filter small aquatic life from the shallow, muddy bottoms of marshes and lagoons. They are scarce but increasing in summer along portions of the Gulf coast. Some birds remain year-round; most migrate south.

Wood Stork

young

young

Roseate
Spoonbill

WHITE HERONS

GREAT EGRET

SNOWY EGRET

Cattle egrets feed inland with livestock, but many nest in coastal colonies established by native herons.

The cattle egret is smaller and stockier than the snowy egret and has a yellow bill. In breeding plumage, it has buff plumes on its head and breast.

An egret is a type of heron. The name comes from the long, showy white plumes, "aigrettes," on birds in breeding plumage. These plumes, prized adornments for women's hats at the time, led to the birds' slaughter and near extinction a century ago.

The snowy and great egrets, the two most persecuted, have made a comeback and frequent coastal marshes north to New England in summer. Most winter in warm Florida and Gulf coast marshes, where food is plentiful. They both feed heavily on fish but take frogs, insects, and other prey.

The great egret is the larger bird, but the sure marks separating all white egrets are bill and leg color. The **great egret** has black legs and a yellow bill. A small area in front of the eyes turns bright green briefly during nesting season.

Snowy egrets have black bills with some yellow in front of the eye. Their legs are also black, but the feet are bright yellow. In young birds, a yellow stripe runs up the back of the legs.

Some dark herons have white forms. Little blue herons (p. 90) are white their first year. They are the size of snowy egrets but have duller bills, greenish legs, and dusky wing tips. In south Florida, there are white forms of the reddish egret (p. 90) and great blue heron (p. 88).

Great Egret

great egret

snowy egret

young

breeding

Snowy Egret

DARK HERONS

GREAT BLUE HERON

TRICOLORED HERON

A white race of the great blue heron lives in southern Florida. Known as the great white heron, it has a yellow bill and yellow legs, which help distinguish it from the great egret shown on the preceding page.

At two feet in length, the tricolored heron is not small, but it is dwarfed by the stately great blue heron. Great blues are widespread on coasts from Texas to the Canadian Maritimes in summer. Many retreat from the northern coasts in winter, but a few hardy individuals survive seemingly impossible winter conditions as far north as Canada. Along the coast, most great blues feed in marshes, but they will forage anywhere there is something edible. They have been known to stalk belly-deep into the surf for fish.

The **great blue heron** is so large that it is sometimes thought to be a crane, but cranes don't have the neck stripes or the black head plumes. Even flying at a distance, the great blue can be separated from cranes. Herons fly with their necks folded; cranes extend theirs.

In winter, most tricolored herons retreat to coasts from the Carolinas south. They are slender, graceful herons that spend much of their time hunting fish. While the great blue heron usually still-hunts or stalks slowly, the tricolored can also be seen chasing and generally employing whatever technique works best.

The **tricolored heron** is the only wading bird with dark upperparts and a white belly. Young birds have a rusty neck.

Great Blue Heron

young

great blue
(on take-off)

Tricolored Heron

young

DARK HERONS

REDDISH EGRET

LITTLE BLUE HERON

Reddish egrets sometimes sprint wildly after fish. They also engage in "canopy feeding"—spreading their wings to cast a shadow, which improves visibility and, perhaps, attracts fish.

Little blue herons are more numerous and widespread than reddish egrets. They can be found on coasts year-round as far north as New Jersey, with small numbers venturing to Maine. They often hunt alone in shadows, unseen. Reddish egrets are scarce and only in a few localities on the Texas and Florida coasts.

In most areas, a small, slender heron that appears almost uniformly dark is a **little blue heron,** but along portions of the Gulf coast, the reddish egret is a possibility; look closely.

Reddish egrets are larger than little blues. The brightness and color of the neck plumes on each vary with the light. The pale eyes and bright cobalt blue leg color are the **reddish egret's** best year-round marks. Little blue herons have dull legs and dark eyes. In breeding plumage, the black-tipped pink bill is a sure mark for the reddish egret. Winter adults and young birds have black bills. The bill is bluish, blending to a dark tip in adult little blue herons.

Both reddish egrets and little blue herons have a white form. Most reddish egrets are dark, but some in Florida are white; the leg and bill colors remain good marks. All little blue herons are white with dusky wing tips for the first year. Their bills resemble an adult's, but the legs are greenish. Molting youngsters look patchy.

Reddish Egret

young

reddish

Little Blue Heron

molting
young

little blue

young

IBISES

WHITE-FACED
IBIS

GLOSSY
IBIS

WHITE IBIS

Ancestors of the
white-faced ibis invad-
ed North America
thousands of years
ago. The glossy ibis
arrived in the 1800s.
Both probably evolved
from the same Old
World species.

Ibises are most notable for their long, curved bills. They feed in marshes and swamps, any area that is covered with only a few inches of water—fresh or salt—or that borders water.

Ibises eat almost any aquatic life they can catch, but their slim, curved bills are a special threat to burrowing crabs and snails. The tips of their bills are sensitive, and most prey is caught by probing.

Adult **white ibises** have brilliant red bills and legs. (During nesting, the outer portion of the bill turns dark.) Young birds are brown above, but their white bellies distinguish them from other ibises. White ibises usually feed in flocks and are sometimes seen in large flocks.

The **white-faced** and **glossy ibises** are very similar. In fact, their winter plumages are nearly identical. Fortunately, ranges of the two species typically overlap only along the western Gulf coast. The red eye of the adult white-faced distinguishes it from the glossy ibis in winter. In breeding plumage, the area around the eye is a good mark but can be seen only at close range or with good binoculars. The skin near the eye is reddish with a border of white feathers in the white-faced. In the glossy ibis, the eye area is dark with a pale bluish white border.

summer glossy

summer white-faced

winter

White-faced and Glossy Ibises

young

White Ibis

molting young

young

STOCKY HERONS

GREEN HERON

YELLOW-CROWNED NIGHT-HERON

BLACK-CROWNED NIGHT-HERON

The American bittern, primarily a freshwater bird, also winters in brackish coastal marshes. It is a secretive bulky brown wader with paler forewings than those of young night-herons.

The night-herons and green heron are bulky birds that often sit hunched up. They are differently shaped than the slender, elegant herons and egrets (see pp. 86-91). And they all feed at night to varying degrees.

The green heron, smallest of the group, is usually seen singly at the edge of still or slow-moving water. It often crouches quietly on limbs or vegetation closely overhanging the water's surface, waiting for small fish. No heron waits more patiently. The upperparts of the **green heron** are actually blue-green. At a distance or in poor light, the bird often looks dark overall except for its bright yellow or orange legs. It gives a loud *kowp!* when disturbed.

Flocks of night-herons roost in trees when not hunting. They hunt singly or in small groups. The black-crowned hunts a variety of aquatic prey. Yellow-crowneds usually stalk crabs and have heavy bills for cracking the shells.

Bill shape is a good mark distinguishing young **yellow-crowned night-herons** from similar young **black-crowneds.** The adults have distinctly different plumages. The yellow-crowned also has longer legs, a mark easily seen at some distance in flight. Little more than the feet of the black-crowned extend beyond its tail; much more of the yellow-crowned's legs show.

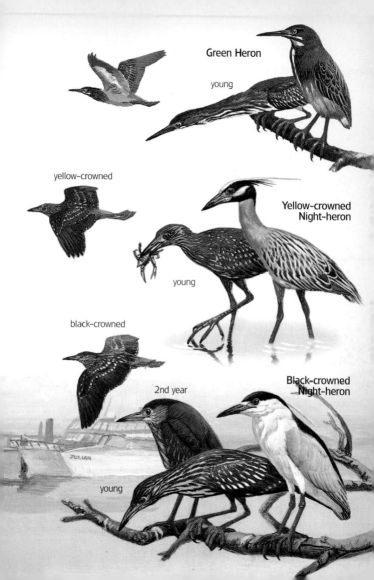

Green Heron

young

yellow-crowned

**Yellow-crowned
Night-heron**

young

black-crowned

**Black-crowned
Night-heron**

2nd year

young

RAILS

SORA

VIRGINIA RAIL

CLAPPER RAIL

King rails are a fresh-water version of the clapper rail. It takes good binoculars and some experience to separate the two except by habitat. Both can occupy brackish marshes.

Rails are shy birds that typically remain hidden in heavy marsh vegetation. High tides sometimes force them from cover. The clapper rail is usually identified by its call, but the sora and Virginia rail call less frequently on their coastal wintering grounds. Rails are seen occasionally in brief flight over a marsh or scampering across openings in the vegetation.

The sora is the most numerous rail. A few nest in coastal marshes in the Northeast, but on most coasts, the sora is seen during migration and in winter—if seen at all. They eat mostly seeds. The best marks for the **sora** are its chicken-like bill and the black mask of the adult.

The long, reddish bill and legs and the black-and-white flanks are good marks for **Virginia rails.** In flight, note the reddish wing patches. Virginia rails feed heavily on insects and small prey. They often share marshes with soras.

Clapper rails are named for their call, a series of percussive notes (*kek-kek-kek-kek-kek-kek-kek,* like a wooden clapper) that start loud and then soften while accelerating. The call is given year-round and is the **clapper rail's** best "mark," providing it comes from a salt-water marsh (see sidebar). Clapper rails are much larger and heavier billed than Virginia rails. They take prey as large as crabs.

young

Sora

young

Virginia Rail

pale form

Clapper Rail

dark form

STILT AND AVOCET

STILT

AVOCET

Both the **stilt** and the **avocet** are striking birds that need little description beyond their illustrations. When either bird is wading, the extreme length of its legs may be concealed, but in flight, the legs trail far beyond the tail. Unfortunately, both birds are scarce to rare along the Gulf and Atlantic coasts away from Texas. They prefer tidal pools or similar shallow water with soft, muddy bottoms.

Avocets once nested along the Atlantic coast north to New Jersey before hunting virtually eliminated them in the East. However, they continue to winter on Gulf and southern Atlantic coasts, and they nest on the southern Texas coast. Some are seen in fall migration along the Atlantic coast.

Avocets' bills are curved, the female's more so than the male's. The birds typically feed by sweeping their bills through bottom mud and catching any small prey that is disturbed. The bill tips are very sensitive to touch. Avocets swim when water is too deep for wading.

Stilts can swim too, but they seldom do so. Stilts usually pick insects or other tiny prey from the surface of still water. Their legs are so long that, on dry land, they can't pick from the ground without crouching. Females have browner backs than males.

Stilt

♂

♀

summer

Avocet

♂

♀

winter

GODWIT AND OYSTERCATCHER

MARBLED GODWIT

AMERICAN OYSTERCATCHER

The Hudsonian godwit has an upturned bill and is scarce on the Atlantic coast in fall migration. Most migrate well offshore without stopping.

The best marks for the Hudsonian godwit are seen in flight—a black-and-white tail, blackish wing linings, and a white wing stripe.

Like the stilt and avocet shown on the preceding page, the **American oyster-catcher** is a "can't miss" identification. And oystercatchers are not that difficult to find on much of the Atlantic coast; they're scarcer along the Gulf. Pairs or small noisy flocks feed on shellfish exposed at low tide in salt marsh or the intertidal zone. Their long, blade-like bills are specialized for the task. At high tide, they gather, often in large flocks, on sandbars or undisturbed beaches to wait until the tide once again exposes the shellfish.

The **marbled godwit** is a jumbo-sized sandpiper with an extraordinarily long bill. Since there aren't many sandpipers as large, identification is not difficult. The whimbrel and long-billed curlew (p. 102) have down-curved, not upturned, bills (also see sidebar). The smaller dowitchers (p. 106) have long, straight bills.

Finding a godwit to identify is the more difficult problem. They winter on coasts but are scarce along the Gulf and on south Atlantic shores. Some are seen in migration, especially in fall, along the Atlantic from Massachusetts south. Once they were as common as some of the smaller sandpipers that scamper along the beach, but they never recovered from hunting in the 1800s.

summer

♂

winter

♀

Marbled Godwit

young

American Oystercatcher

WHIMBREL AND CURLEW

WHIMBREL

LONG-BILLED CURLEW

The Eskimo curlew's story is tragic. It is not illustrated because it probably no longer exists. A bit smaller than a whimbrel, it was abundant in migration but easy to shoot.

Some birds survived the hunting, but the species seems to have since disappeared. Hopeful birders still watch the Texas coast in spring.

Their size and down-curved bills distinguish **whimbrels** and **long-billed curlews** from other shorebirds. The same features usually can be used to separate them from each other. If in doubt, check the head for dark stripes; only the whimbrel has them. In flight, the bright cinnamon underwings of the long-billed curlew are a good mark.

Whimbrels were wary enough to survive the unrestricted hunting of the 1800s, but the long-billed curlew is another sad story. In the East, it can be expected only on the Texas coast in winter. It once migrated in fall along the Atlantic from New Jersey south.

The long-billed curlew is the largest sandpiper. Females are slightly larger than males and have longer bills. Young birds' bills are about the size of a whimbrel's. With the long bill, the curlew can feed at many levels in the intertidal zone.

Whimbrels are most numerous in migration (spring; late summer and fall) along the Gulf and on the Atlantic coast from New Jersey south. Some remain throughout the winter from the Carolinas south. Whimbrels usually feed in the intertidal zone at low tide, especially on mudflats, but during migration, they might be found anywhere along the coast. Crabs are a favorite food.

102

Whimbrel

Long-billed Curlew

young ♂

WILLET AND YELLOWLEGS

LESSER YELLOWLEGS

GREATER YELLOWLEGS

WILLET

The solitary sandpiper is much like the lesser yellowlegs (including the bobbing motion) but is smaller, has dark legs, and a dark rump. It is a freshwater bird that sometimes visits bays and inlets in migration.

The willet is fairly numerous along the Gulf and Atlantic coasts. It is usually the largest shorebird on the beach, towering over the little surf-chasers. It also forages in marshes and other coastal habitats, taking prey as large as crabs.

Seen standing, a **willet** is a big, nondescript, gray-brown sandpiper with pale blue-gray legs and bill. When flushed, it reveals the dramatic white wing stripes that are its best mark. Willets are usually seen singly or in small groups. They sometimes swim in tidal pools or deep marsh.

Bright yellow legs distinguish the yellowlegs from other coastal sandpipers. Bill length and calls are the best marks separating the **greater yellowlegs** from the **lesser.** The greater's bill is half again its head length and slightly upturned; the lesser's is about the length of its head and perfectly straight. Greater yellowlegs give a ringing flight call of three to five notes; the lesser's call is flatter and usually one- or two-noted.

Both yellowlegs feed actively, often bobbing their heads or tails. They don't probe with their bills, but pick minnows, bugs, and other small prey from near the water's surface or at the edges of coastal marshes and tide pools.

willet

Lesser
Yellowlegs

yellowlegs (lesser)

summer

winter

Greater
Yellowlegs

summer

winter

Willet

KNOT AND DOWITCHERS

RED KNOT

SHORT-BILLED
DOWITCHER

LONG-BILLED
DOWITCHER

Knots depend on a few specific sites with reliable food sources in migration. Once abundant, they are now steadily declining with disruption of their coastal stopover points.

Knots and dowitchers are chunky sandpipers, as are the three birds in the next illustration. Their shapes help distinguish them from longer-necked, more slender sandpipers.

Flocks of knots migrate along the coast in spring and fall. Long-distance migrants, most winter in South America and nest in the Arctic. Some remain on the mudflats and beaches of the southern Atlantic and Gulf in winter.

In spring, their robin-red breasts distinguish **red knots** from all except the dowitchers, which have longer bills. In winter, their size and pale plumage distinguish them from everything except dowitchers and black-bellied plovers (p. 110), all of which have distinctive bills and rump and tail patterns.

Dowitchers feed openly in flocks on mudflats and in shallow pools using a rapid vertical "stitching" motion. Snipes, the only similar long-billed bird (p. 108), are wary and usually solitary. There are two dowitcher species. **Short-billed dowitchers** are fairly numerous on the Gulf and Atlantic coasts. **Long-billed dowitchers** are scarce in the East, especially on salt water, but sometimes are seen with short-bills. Bill length is not a reliable mark separating the two; flight calls are. Short-bills give a mellow *tu-tu-tu;* long-bills, a thin, high-pitched *keek.*

Red Knot

winter

young

summer

knot

dowitcher

Dowitchers

winter

young
short-billed

typical summer
short-billed

SANDPIPERS

SNIPE

PURPLE SANDPIPER

RUDDY TURNSTONE

Snipes are yet another species that was once abundant but hunted to scarcity. It is speculated that more snipes have been shot than any other shorebird.

Like the dowitchers shown on the preceding page, snipes have long bills. However, a **snipe's** plumage is darker than a dowitcher's, and snipes usually feed secretively and singly at marsh edges rather than openly in flocks on mudflats. They are most often seen at dusk or dawn. When alarmed, they take off in rapid zigzag flight, giving a harsh *scaip* call.

The purple sandpiper and ruddy turnstone forage on rocky shores and jetties in winter, inspecting seaweed and rock crevices for bugs or other small life. Turnstones also visit beaches, where they often probe in the beach wrack with their stubby, slightly upturned bills. And they sometimes forage in marshes and inlets.

Purple sandpipers winter farther north on the Atlantic than any other sandpiper. They are fairly numerous, usually staying in small flocks. Dark gray describes their color better than purple. Their best mark is the thin, slightly drooped bill. The base of the bill is yellow or orange-yellow, as are the legs.

There is nothing subtle about the **ruddy turnstone's** summer plumage. The brown bib is a good mark in winter. Even better is the "harlequin" back pattern seen in flight. Fairly numerous, turnstones are usually in small flocks, often with other small shorebirds.

Snipe

snipe

purple
sandpiper

summer

Purple
Sandpiper

winter

ruddy turnstone

summer

Ruddy
Turnstone

winter

PLOVERS

BLACK–BELLIED PLOVER

KILLDEER

SEMIPALMATED PLOVER

American golden-plovers are seen in spring migration (many still in molt) on the Texas coast. They resemble the black-bellied but have gold-speckled upperparts and no black wing pit.

Plovers are different from sandpipers. They have distinctive short, pigeon-like bills, slightly swollen at the tip. Many have at least partial neck bands. Most feed on mudflats and sandy beaches in a distinctive stop–and–go fashion. They run a short way, abruptly pause to pick at food, then look about and scamper off again. They don't probe into the ground as sandpipers do, but pick from the surface.

The black–bellied plover and killdeer are about the size of the sandpipers shown on the preceding pages. The two black neck bands are sure marks for the **killdeer.** In flight, the orange back and rump are obvious. Killdeer are scarce along the coast, most often seen on dry flats.

Black-bellied plovers are often seen on beaches and mudflats in winter and during migration. The winter plumage is pale, with contrasting dark eyes, bill, and legs. The striking summer plumage is seen in spring migration. In flight, the black wing pits are a sure mark.

The **semipalmated plover** is similar to the small plovers (p. 112). It is the only one with both a dark back—like wet sand—and a small bill. Also note the orange legs, the breast band, and the head markings. In winter and during migration, the semipalmated is fairly numerous in flocks on wet sand or mudflats.

Black-bellied Plover

young   summer   winter

black-
bellied

semi-
palmated

Killdeer

winter

summer   **Semipalmated
Plover**

PLOVERS

SNOWY PLOVER

WILSON'S PLOVER

PIPING PLOVER

PLUV-er is the preferred pronunciation over *PLOH-ver.*

The small plovers in this illustration are all scarce and declining. They are disappearing because the sandy beaches they use for feeding and nesting are the same ones that people use for recreation. The semipalmated plover shown on the previous page is much more numerous than snowy, Wilson's, or piping plovers because it nests in the remote Arctic.

Snowy plovers are spottily distributed along the Gulf coast, usually in small flocks except when nesting. They like the dry sand above the high water line, although they often feed at the edge of the surf. Their pale backs blend into a dry-sand background so well that **snowy plovers** are hard to see even when nearby. Note the thin black bill, dark legs, and incomplete collar.

The heavy black bill of **Wilson's plover** is its best mark. The bill is large enough to subdue fiddler crabs. Other small plovers eat mostly insects. Wilson's is usually seen alone or in pairs. It is fairly tame and slow moving.

There are fewer than 2,500 pairs of piping plovers. A few beaches are reserved and protected for their nesting in order to help maintain some populations. The **piping plover** has a very pale back like the snowy but a stubbier bill and orange legs. It often gives a clear, piping, *peep-lo* call.

summer

Snowy Plover

winter

snowy

Wilson's

piping

summer ♂

Wilson's Plover

♀ and winter

summer

winter

Piping Plover

SANDPIPERS

PECTORAL SANDPIPER

SPOTTED SANDPIPER

STILT SANDPIPER

The stilt sandpiper is shown on the Arctic tundra where it nests.

Wilson's phalarope (9") is occasionally seen on pools in brackish and salt marshes. A long, needle-thin bill and white rump (seen in flight) are good marks.

This illustration shows some of the scarcer small sandpipers. The pectoral and stilt sandpipers are seen briefly in migration, usually in late summer or fall. The spotted sandpiper is more often present on shores but is seldom on open beaches or mudflats.

The first marks noticed in a **spotted sandpiper** are that it teeters when it walks, and it walks alone (rarely with others). It stalks the water's edge taking almost any small prey. The spotted breast is a sure plumage mark in spring and summer; in winter, note the white wedge between the dark wing and the dark side of the breast. When disturbed, spotted sandpipers fly close to the water and usually return quickly to shore. They glide on distinctive bowed, quivering wings interrupted with shallow wing beats.

The pectoral sandpiper is usually seen on grassy salt marsh edges, often singly among other shorebirds. It is dark brown and suggests a larger version of the least sandpiper (p. 118). The **pectoral sandpiper's** best mark is the way its breast streaks end sharply at the belly.

The long legs, drooped bill, and white eyebrow are good marks for the **stilt sandpiper** in any plumage. They are best seen in fall migration, often in muddy waters feeding with dowitchers (p. 106). Some winter on the Texas coast.

114

winter

summer

Pectoral Sandpiper

summer

winter

Spotted
Sandpiper

winter

summer

Stilt
Sandpiper

SANDPIPERS

DUNLIN

SANDERLING

Bill, legs, and points of structure are often easier and more certain marks than plumage in shorebirds—indeed, in all birds. The variery of plumages due to season, age, and the molting process can make plumage identification complicated

The sandpipers in this illustration and the next are the little ones seen seasonally on beaches and mudflats. All nest in the Arctic, but even in late June and July, there are often some migrants on Atlantic shores.

To sort them out, start with the sanderling. Chances are good that any small flock of sandpipers scampering along the surf on a sandy beach is mostly, if not all, sanderlings.

In fall and winter, the **sanderling** is the palest of the small sandpipers; its black bill and legs offer noticeable contrast. Young birds (Aug.-Sept.) have distinctive black-spotted backs. In May, the upperparts, head, and breast become rusty brown, and black spots show on the back. In flight, note the broad white wing stripe.

Dunlin are numerous on mudflats. Note the drooped bill. Only the stilt sandpiper shown on the preceding page has a bill like the **dunlin's,** and the stilt sandpiper has long greenish legs, not short black ones. Dunlin in winter are a darker gray-brown above than sanderlings, and a dark wash extends onto their necks and breasts. In fall, some bright young birds might be seen still molting into dull winter plumage. Spring birds are bright reddish above and sport unmistakable black belly patches.

116

winter

molting young

Dunlin

summer

dunlin

sanderling

Sanderling

young

winter

summer

SANDPIPERS

SEMIPALMATED
SANDPIPER

WESTERN
SANDPIPER

LEAST
SANDPIPER

Baird's and white-
rumped sandpipers
are scarce coastal
migrants. The white-
rumped does, indeed,
have an all-white
rump, and both have
long wings that extend
beyond the tail on
standing birds, a good
mark separating them
from other peeps.

Known as "peeps," the semipalmated, western, and least sandpipers are all smaller than the sanderling (p. 116), and in fall and winter, they are all slightly darker. Peeps are sometimes found on sandy beaches with sanderlings, but they prefer muddy shores, marshes, and tide flats. They often feed together in flocks, with the least sandpiper tending toward the upper margins of the mudflats.

The **least sandpiper** is the smallest sandpiper in the world. It is the darkest brown, especially on the breast in winter. The yellow legs are a good mark year-round, but they can be darkened by mud. Also note the small thin bill. Least sandpipers are not as numerous as the other peeps but are the most common ones on US shores in winter.

The western sandpiper is scarce on most North American shores in winter, and the semipalmated is virtually absent by October. Both are abundant migrants, however. In spring, the **western sandpiper** is brighter than the **semipalmated,** with reddish marks on the face, crown, and wings. Its breast streaks extend well down the sides. In fall, both adults are dull gray (darker than the sanderling, lighter than the least sandpiper) and often stump the experts. The longer bill of the western seen in the illustration is not a sure mark; bill length varies.

118

western and
semipalmated

least

summer

**Semipalmated
Sandpiper**

winter

summer

**Western
Sandpiper**

young

**Least
Sandpiper**

winter

summer

Belted Kingfisher

♂ ♀

KINGFISHER

BELTED
KINGFISHER

There is one coastal waterbird that feeds like no other, the kingfisher. It plunge-dives for fish like some aerialists, but it doesn't glide over water searching for them. It waits on a perch beside still or slow-moving water for fish to appear. Kingfishers often hover before plunging for prey.

As one would expect because of its unique foraging style, the **belted kingfisher** looks quite different than other waterbirds. Note the large head and bill and the thick crest. Females have a rusty breast band lacking in males. Kingfishers are noisy and conspicuous. They are fairly numerous in coastal marshes and estuaries year-round on most of the Atlantic and Gulf coasts.

INDEX AND CHECK-LIST

How many species of birds have you identified? Keeping a record is the only way to know. Sooner or later, even the most casual bird-watcher makes notes of the species seen on a trip or in a day. People keep backyard lists, year lists, state lists, every kind of checklist. All serious birders maintain a life list. Seeing your life list grow can become part of the pleasure of bird-watching. The pages that follow are designed to serve as your checklist of coastal waterbirds as well as an index to their illustrations in this guide.

English names used in this guide and listed in the index are the familiar names used in common conversation. For the most part, they are the same as the formal English names adopted by the American Ornithologists' Union in the seventh edition of their *Check-list of North American Birds,* 1998. When the formal AOU English name differs from the common name used in this guide, the AOU English name is given on the second line of the index entry.

The Latin names in italics are the AOU's scientific names.

✓ Species	Date	Location

AVOCET　98
American Avocet
Recurvirostra americana

BRANT　56
Branta bernicla

BUFFLEHEAD　76
Bucephala albeola

CANVASBACK　72
Aythya valisineria

COOT　80
American Coot
Fulica americana

DOUBLE-CRESTED **C**ORMORANT　60
Phalacrocorax auritus

GREAT **C**ORMORANT　60
Phalacrocorax carbo

LONG-BILLED **C**URLEW　102
Numenius americanus

LONG-BILLED **D**OWITCHER　106
Limnodromus scolopaceus

SHORT-BILLED **D**OWITCHER　106
Limnodromus griseus

BLACK **D**UCK　64
American Black Duck
Anas rubripes

MOTTLED **D**UCK　64
Anas fulvigula

RING-NECKED **D**UCK　70
Aythya collaris

RUDDY **D**UCK　72
Oxyura jamaicensis

DUNLIN　116
Calidris alpina

GREAT **E**GRET　86
Ardea alba

✔ Species		Date	Location
○ REDDISH **E**GRET *Egretta rufescens*	90		
○ SNOWY **E**GRET *Egretta thula*	86		
○ COMMON **E**IDER *Somateria mollissima*	74		
○ KING **E**IDER *Somateria spectabilis*	74		
○ MAGNIFICENT **F**RIGATEBIRD *Fregata magnificens*	32		
○ **G**ADWALL *Anas strepera*	66		
○ **G**ANNET Northern Gannet *Morus bassanus*	30		
○ MARBLED **G**ODWIT *Limosa fedoa*	100		
○ COMMON **G**OLDENEYE *Bucephala clangula*	76		
○ CANADA **G**OOSE *Branta canadensis*	56		
○ SNOW **G**OOSE *Chen caerulescens*	54		
○ WHITE-FRONTED **G**OOSE Greater White-fronted Goose *Anser albifrons*	54		
○ HORNED **G**REBE *Podiceps auritus*	82		
○ PIED-BILLED **G**REBE *Podilymbus podiceps*	82		
○ RED-NECKED **G**REBE *Podiceps grisegena*	82		
○ BLACK **G**UILLEMOT *Cepphus grylle*	62		

✓ Species		Date	Location
◯ BONAPARTE'S **G**ULL *Larus philadelphia*	40	....	....
◯ GLAUCOUS **G**ULL *Larus hyperboreus*	36	....	....
◯ GREAT BLACK-BACKED **G**ULL *Larus marinus*	34	....	....
◯ HERRING **G**ULL *Larus argentatus*	38	....	....
◯ ICELAND **G**ULL *Larus glaucoides*	36	....	....
◯ LAUGHING **G**ULL *Larus atricilla*	40	....	....
◯ RING-BILLED **G**ULL *Larus delawarensis*	38	....	....
◯ GREAT BLUE **H**ERON *Ardea herodias*	88	....	....
◯ GREEN **H**ERON *Butorides virescens*	94	....	....
◯ LITTLE BLUE **H**ERON *Egretta caerulea*	90	....	....
◯ TRICOLORED **H**ERON *Egretta tricolor*	88	....	....
◯ GLOSSY **I**BIS *Plegadis falcinellus*	92	....	....
◯ WHITE **I**BIS *Eudocimus albus*	92	....	....
◯ WHITE-FACED **I**BIS *Plegadis chihi*	92	....	....
◯ PARASITIC **J**AEGER *Stercorarius parasiticus*	30	....	....
◯ **K**ILLDEER *Charadrius vociferus*	110	....	....
◯ BELTED **K**INGFISHER *Ceryle alcyon*	120	....	....

✓ Species		Date	Location
◯ RED **K**NOT *Calidris canutus*	106		
◯ COMMON **L**OON *Gavia immer*	58		
◯ RED–THROATED **L**OON *Gavia stellata*	58		
◯ **M**ALLARD *Anas platyrhynchos*	64		
◯ RED–BREASTED **M**ERGANSER *Mergus serrator*	80		
◯ BLACK–CROWNED **N**IGHT-HERON *Nycticorax nycticorax*	94		
◯ YELLOW–CROWNED **N**IGHT-HERON *Nyctanassa violacea*	94		
◯ **O**LDSQUAW *Clangula hyemalis*	76		
◯ AMERICAN **O**YSTERCATCHER *Haematopus palliatus*	100		
◯ BROWN **P**ELICAN *Pelecanus occidentalis*	32		
◯ WHITE **P**ELICAN American White Pelican *Pelecanus erythrorhynchos*	52		
◯ **P**INTAIL Northern Pintail *Anas acuta*	66		
◯ BLACK–BELLIED **P**LOVER *Pluvialis squatarola*	110		
◯ PIPING **P**LOVER *Charadrius melodus*	112		
◯ SNOWY **P**LOVER *Charadrius alexandrinus*	112		
◯ SEMIPALMATED **P**LOVER *Charadrius semipalmatus*	110		

✓ Species	Date	Location
◯ WILSON'S PLOVER *Charadrius wilsonia*	112	
◯ CLAPPER RAIL *Rallus longirostris*	96	
◯ VIRGINIA RAIL *Rallus limicola*	96	
◯ RAZORBILL *Alca torda*	62	
◯ REDHEAD *Aythya americana*	72	
◯ SANDERLING *Calidris alba*	116	
◯ LEAST SANDPIPER *Calidris minutilla*	118	
◯ PECTORAL SANDPIPER *Calidris melanotos*	114	
◯ PURPLE SANDPIPER *Calidris maritima*	108	
◯ SEMIPALMATED SANDPIPER *Calidris pusilla*	118	
◯ SPOTTED SANDPIPER *Actitis macularia*	114	
◯ STILT SANDPIPER *Calidris himantopus*	114	
◯ WESTERN SANDPIPER *Calidris mauri*	118	
◯ GREATER SCAUP *Aythya marila*	70	
◯ LESSER SCAUP *Aythya affinis*	70	
◯ BLACK SCOTER *Melanitta nigra*	78	
◯ SURF SCOTER *Melanitta perspicillata*	78	

✓ Species		Date	Location
○ **WHITE-WINGED SCOTER** *Melanitta fusca*	78		
○ **SHOVELER** Northern Shoveler *Anas clypeata*	68		
○ **BLACK SKIMMER** *Rynchops niger*	34		
○ **SNIPE** Common Snipe *Gallinago gallinago*	108		
○ **SORA** *Porzana carolina*	96		
○ **ROSEATE SPOONBILL** *Ajaia ajaja*	84		
○ **STILT** Black-necked Stilt *Himantopus mexicanus*	98		
○ **WOOD STORK** *Mycteria americana*	84		
○ **WILSON'S STORM-PETREL** *Oceanites oceanicus*	30		
○ **MUTE SWAN** *Cygnus olor*	52		
○ **TUNDRA SWAN** *Cygnus columbianus*	52		
○ **BLUE-WINGED TEAL** *Anas discors*	68		
○ **GREEN-WINGED TEAL** *Anas crecca*	68		
○ **BLACK TERN** *Chlidonias niger*	50		
○ **CASPIAN TERN** *Sterna caspia*	44		
○ **COMMON TERN** *Sterna hirundo*	46		

✓ Species		Date	Location
◯ FORSTER'S TERN *Sterna forsteri*	46		
◯ GULL-BILLED TERN *Sterna nilotica*	48		
◯ LEAST TERN *Sterna antillarum*	50		
◯ ROYAL TERN *Sterna maxima*	44		
◯ SANDWICH TERN *Sterna sandvicensis*	48		
◯ RUDDY TURNSTONE *Arenaria interpres*	108		
◯ GREATER YELLOWLEGS *Tringa melanoleuca*	104		
◯ LESSER YELLOWLEGS *Tringa flavipes*	104		
◯ WHIMBREL *Numenius phaeopus*	102		
◯ AMERICAN WIGEON *Anas americana*	66		
◯ WILLET *Catoptrophorus semipalmatus*	104		